STUMBLING IN THE BLOOM

Also by John Pass

Taking Place, 1971
The Kenojuak Prints, 1973
AIR 18, 1973
Port of Entry, 1975
Love's Confidence, 1976
Blossom: An Accompaniment, 1978
There Go The Cars, 1979
An Arbitrary Dictionary, 1984
Rugosa, 1991
The Hour's Acropolis, 1991
Radical Innocence, 1994
Mud Bottom, 1996
Water Stair, 2000
nowrite.doc, 2004

Stumbling In The Bloom

John Pass

OOLICHAN BOOKS
LANTZVILLE, BRITISH COLUMBIA, CANADA
2005

Library and Archives Canada Cataloguing in Publication

Pass, John, 1947-
Stumbling in the bloom / John Pass.

Poems
ISBN 0-88982-201-8

I. Title.
PS8581.A77S88 2005   C811'.54   C2005-900667-6

We gratefully acknowledge the support of the Canada Council for the Arts, the BC Ministry of Tourism, Small Business and Culture, and the Government of Canada through the Book Publishing Industry Development Program, for our publishing activities.

Cover image courtesy of Carmen Elliot.

Published by
Oolichan Books
P.O. Box 10
Lantzville, BC
V0R 2H0

Printed in Canada

What wond'rous Life in this I lead!
Ripe Apples drop about my head;
The Luscious Clusters of the Vine
Upon my Mouth do crush their Wine;
The Nectarine, and curious Peach,
Into my hands themselves do reach;
Stumbling on Melons, as I pass,
Ensnar'd with Flow'rs, I fall on Grass.

Andrew Marvell
The Garden

Alone with our madness and favorite flower
We see that there really is nothing left to write about.
Or rather, it is necessary to write about the same old things
In the same way, repeating the same things over and over
For love to continue and be gradually different.

John Ashbery
Late Echo

Contents

III Idiot Of Place

IV Wind Chime

I

Trumpet Vine

Raspberries, Roses

Come into the huge and intractable beauty
of what I thought I knew, dumbfounded

at the lucent breadth
of uninhabited context, immense locality

where self's wisp (just reminded) whispers, *oh*
the terrible artifice of human thought.
I was at that creek-mouth

of which I had written and remembered
so much . . . all sloughed away, overwhelmed
in an instant was the desperate, puny array

of particulars. But for their history so belittled
or because of that (my surprised relief)
I was satisfied, speechless. But eager to say

what it was gave body, tradition, happiness, depth
of field to the moment you'll appreciate

my difficulty. Later I looked at the fingerless palms
of nasturtium leaves outstretched from a low planter

with needy recognition, a stupefied receiving presence
out of hand as on the first day

of summer vacation I turned away
from the raspberries, roses, reaching
under the sky's blue bowl
for mine.

nowrite.doc

"Trying to whisper life came back, *the light came back."*

—Jorie Graham

Morning of the night waking in the middle finally to myself must begin
the writing-against-not-writing entries to find feeling I look out into
the upper corner of the yard the opening towards the bush, false path
sun in the long wet grass, early sun, first sun just up over Hallowell
and the standing there blank in my head splashed bright, hopeful.

The full green of everything early summer stuffed
with rain-flushed soil and now sun. Say straight out
it's too much the massed salal around stumps in the orchard, lemon balm
blocking the raspberry path, roses hanging above the door, head-turning
whiff of honeysuckle like a lover's skin intoxicating in the dark, mauve wands
of fireweed my height out the kitchen window. Too much, even not taking
my eyes off the keyboard, not going back. Even conceding

that to pushy process dumb luck its confrontation
invites despair, despair confronting the unmanageable
beauty, the unconstrained beauty no strategy no trope no tone
gets true. Or buoyed up on the leafy shining wave with bright yellow
sunclustered St John's Wort I tossed weeds and trimmings past, pullings
from the patio edges hosing it down after, rose petals falling
behind me on wet cement . . .

***

A feast it was to be a long table laden, friends its length
as at home and witty and flamboyant as pots of scented
(pineapple, orange) geranium: evolved, steeped

in the resins of long congeniality and playful mutant
opportunity. I made a note: High Ground, the table
set. And this is it. This is it. Make no mistake about it. This
book in pieces: real life love life dream earth.
You decide which is what goes where.

The bee was there stumbling in the huge bloom the fibre-optic-like display
of leggy, yellow, orange-tipped stamens. Stumbling, no method, but laden
its orange leg-sacs. And a thousand blooms to go after that one.

***

Precision of the spin of my son's bicycle wheel
where he works on it upturned on the porch
catches my eye. A precision that pleases, the quick
ticking over glint of sunlight in the spokes, then

                              on a dime! The new brakes!
I love the skill that makes that smooth, a companion
to living, being able

to fix things, the toilet for example:
the clog clears tho' the metal snake balked, twisted
back on itself, grinding porcelain and the baking soda and vinegar fizz
was unconvincing and the hot water blast from the hose stuck in there
flushed back nothing. But somehow

it gets cleared, goes clear, flushes! And the mind likes that
clarity got to via ingenious paraphernalia and sensible tools ultimately
proving useless as something else solves but only after knowing how, after effort.
Dumb effort poking about in the sumpy dark trying to think just past seeing
what's in there, where

in the labyrinth despite no evidence (mercifully sometimes no feedback evidence) then eureka flow out of nowhere, through.

***

I come round to my swimming spot past the newly graded little beach
(a couple of loads of sand trucked in and washed away each season)
the huge cedars along the shore path backlit with low sun and shining lake.
A wider path, the roots gnarled and larger over it and the mossy
almost tent-sized, almost level, height of rock

where I first camped thirty years ago, the trees' old scars healed welts
of bark now no-one hacks at them any more. This is park now.

And the water below changeless tho' constantly replenished like the phosphorus
I read in the brain is renewed every two years, the same thoughts burning
running on new fuel in new light.

The water a light oil or liquid silk over my arms and shoulders
as I backstroke and loll. Unchanged and beautiful. Have I said beautiful?
Here we are again. Nostalgia a short walk for everyone but not easy
that the world is beautiful. My good fortune, good mood, relatively
privileged and happy life notwithstanding it is first of all that the world
is beautiful and demanding in its changes and constancies, shades and textures,
crevices in the rock my feet rediscover every summer climbing out

of the different water, and out of work and rain and aches and pains into that fullest
realization again of the world's beauty. I say it over and over without irony or edge
because I'm afraid I might complete my life in a privacy of this knowledge
no-one knowing that I knew, had always known but never said straight out
what I started with but is not easy. Stops me sometimes.

For almost a year, for example, coming to this writing.
It is beauty so complete and complex and aloof and light-footed
I often feel useless and burdened before it. My skills are useless but oblige me to try.
And I cannot shy into the secondary obligation it suggests

to many: social responsibility. It is not social. The beauty in relationships yes
an instance only. Everyone knows this and keeps it, the awkward
human secret: beauty beyond us in the first place,
not some idiosyncrasy of human perception.

    At the party the sun set over the sea in tapestries, transparencies
    of shifting light and colour. Everyone gathered on the beach.
    I'll get Irene. She does water-colours.

    Where's the camera? Everyone awed and a little uneasy.

Now the sun is a couple of fingers above the low
slump of the saddle of mountains across the lake. Dead centre due west.
I sit on my rock, drying off, looking straight out. We smile at each other.

***

All over the garden and near the garden those Garden-of-Eden-shades-of-magenta
bloom holds to wild, or reverts to, left to itself,
are dominant in hard-hack, fireweed, fox-glove, wild-pea and sweet.

Under a cascading surf of perennial geranium true geranium I bumped the mower
feeling for the hidden row of border stones, rough delineation, edge
to track and come back from, blades intact.

Magentas below and greys/whites in cloudy overcast, chickadees
scrabbling for ants and woodbugs in the eavestroughs.
Ice-cream buckets of raspberries to pick. Nowhere to go.

***

Full moon floating in the clear warm air. A moon you really could
read by, only a few stars surviving in pale-lit atmosphere. Rare summer moon
floating, sailing we say of those wondrous moments journeying beyond.
The lake is clear and warm in high summer, I told my distant friend
to tempt him to visit . . .

***

                    Wasps sip sleepily at lake edge
under the heavy scent of fir and cedar and forest earth in the heat.
Even these fierce and quick-tempered mildly seek the water. Carriers?

They go and arrive. In the orchard I take the sweating hose to each tree.
Then sit in the shade, waiting for enough water to soak down. Or stand
with the water trickling at my feet to reach up and thin the apples and pears
tossing the blighted, shrivelled ones so the rest have room to plump but not break
the boughs with so much weight. Everything is risen, suspended and reaching

for the ground. Half-awake in the pre-dawn undefended a nudge
of touchstone feeling, not to be easily accounted for

in daylight, not personal: bereft.

***

World might turn or wait on a word the few days from July
into August, orange berries all of a sudden on the mountain ash.
Sheet lightning all night. But it's never the exact word, never knows
for sure what's coming. A premonition of shift only, antithesis
speaks, and is patient, apprehensive. Doubled over

with kidney stones, then afloat on Demerol and NSAIDs
I'm out in the piss-warm water to my drift log, its smooth surface
a pleasure to my hands. And back on land the granite ledge is perfect
to sun on, a patch of shade for my head under a lucky spangle of fir bough.
Last year my daughter dove here incessantly. *Rate me,* she'd shriek, *rate me!*
8.3 Your knees bent. But better. Nearly 14 now she eases in.

It's pretty cold. Can we go? Where was this leading?
Through heavy air, dew condensed on the big leaves, a loon
then a single raven making its *klook klook* call like water, lonely
as though our friend who knew them, all their words, dead two years, passed over.
Must of vegetation dried out, then dampened, from the pile of garden weedings.

***

Now I am walking under the huge sheltering hands of maple leaves
in my habitual funk. That I can't do things justice, am merely
under, undeserving. Does anyone understand this?
Anguish, and chagrin at the arrogance. Who is equal
even to true rendition? Who lives up to the world's beauty?

Shelter! Such conceit. And such a conceit. Like the fig-leaves of religious painters.
But this shame not sexual hiding. More fundamental
even than that. More human.

Where was this leading? Where gravity and water take the stone.
Well, yeah. Down. Dissolution. Death.

The mauves again, paler magentas. Second flush of wisteria, first windflowers.
And everywhere at the dusty edges unmown sinewy oregano in tiny purplish bloom.
All paler, pattern and colour bleached out

like the patio tablecloth left on through the hot spell.
And leached light behind the vines.

I've been through this before. Of course I have. So have you.
I want to get down and lie on the ground. So I do.

There is nothing taller
than what I don't know.

***

                    Hell is not a place
says the Pope for the Millennium, putting him at the forefront
of 17th century thought. And the radio expert says the existentialists
aren't right either with their *hell is other people* rejoinder.

He's sure Hell is human absence; community
is Heaven. Also inadequate. Surely everything

comes into it. In and out of all of it. But for simplicity
I'm partial to a man, a woman, a garden: the dimensions
of its presence, theirs. In either case. In both places.
Or just the garden and wild

imagination. Till death do them . . . Death ends

distinction. Yes, even our pet dualities dissolve. I fear it
not for myself but for selfish reasons. It will take my loved ones.
Hell's portal is diminishment, our pact with grief made in any Heaven.

***

Clean the chimney! Here is a small panel
of yellow cedar and pine I just made for the hole in the wall to the water tank.
My son is anxious about going away in the fall. I remember

tight with loneliness the bus-ride onto campus each morning the September
I was seventeen. My new briefcase. My Beatle jacket.
Is this helpful? The anecdote?

I tell him anyway. Though the story is never the point.
And the point is never the poem's best pleasure.
Immediately coming back to life, life's elusiveness

is emphatic, demanding. And I'm talking about language.
A dangerous sign. *Yield?* To serendipity, pun doodle:
as *no write.doc* I saved this then thought *now, rite doc?*
Right now I'm feeling better thanks, at sea, despite this sad

header down the immediacy menu. Clownish default/reboot. Save as select all
sun in the window steam off the wet cedar railings radio mumbling . . .
Select as the nasturtium turns sunward
all bright-eyed leaf and flower

and still falter. A critic mentioned
my hesitations. Another deplored that I constantly
undercut my best effects. The snippy ironic cleverness

I wanted no more of
has me by the short and curlies.

Sorry. So sorry! If I'd had the nerve I'd have tried
advertising. I'd have a decent portfolio now. Not the same old briefcase
stuffed with last year's drafts and first lines and punch-
lines and short its stubby closing strap. No snap.

***

Don't forget to smell the roses she gestures taking me
to the pot of dense white bloom fresh-cut on the table
leaning close her fingertip easing a petal aside *why is it*
do you think? That tiny blush of pink in the bud?
And seems surprised as I grasp her waist nuzzle her neck breathing
I love the smell of your hair, it smells like home and has to get back
to making jam writing her novel watering the tomatoes wriggling away.
My beautiful, brilliant wife. I wake up thinking of a single flower

I could bring her. I think of bringing her a single flower.
Which could it be? Jars of peach jam the colour
of bottled sunlight crowd the kitchen counters. Tomorrow friends
arrive from afar. Our son leaves. There's no bloom so full

it could say my piece. Voluptuous fragility. A dewy, messy
tenderness. Lusty musk odour. All the colours. Taste of rain.
Vivacity and integrity in the air. My peace . . . hah!

***

My peace is undiscovered in the perfect day, days of September clarity,
refreshment of the pinks in the papery petunias, oranges in the nasturtiums.
It's a secret in the ripening grapes, cool constellations, Vega's blue-
green, breezes, showers. It slips under my caress, in hand
in a swimming moment's shine

off eye-level lake-water as I shift
to stroke towards shore, as that shadow

of high land holds hollow on the island, a perfectly earthy non-
territorial pleasure. It falls into place as a lucky word, a loving kiss

while fucking, the mesh of desire and affection. My peace falls
into place near perfection, is nearly there. And I would be the poet
of those places wholly. I would give them away

in restlessness, rest, to have them certain.
Certain? That one thing or the other? No!
Subtlety, shading, is the tang

and the tomato. Peace and perfection, the little fishes
nibbling my toes, the lake to myself after Labour Day.
I'm easing in at the beach, the water too cold for diving
and the fishes are tickling my toes where I've disturbed

the sandy bottom, stirred up something
organic they are eating. Through the clear water I watch them
in immense, unsummoned satisfaction, joy. And then swim

luxuriously back and forth, lie down in the sun's luxury, go home
to Maui ribs for dinner, my daughter's birthday favourite . . .

***

On a morning of cloudy damp I stay in
to write of the sunny, breezy days straddling the equinox
I spent on the roof. Oh I was courageous walking there first

with my hammer to drive back the upstart nails in the shakes, wind-lifted.
I looked out and down, down and over. I stood with the hose and drove its shining

lance into every crevice in every rank
of shakes, harrying the crumbling pillows of moss

down-slope over the edges, unseating impacted mats of fir needles becoming
soil against the cedar. I want clean surface for the rain, as clear a run

as its sound is thunder in downpour. I want it near and knifing
when it comes and a slick roof

worthy of its manna, what's due felt full and shed directly. I sit
in the wet for fear of slipping towards the end, at the eastern eaves
pleased tho' the sun leans away
and has angled

the peak's cold shadow in my direction.

***

Late potatoes turned up in a second digging (connective plants and roots
long pulled and composted) miscellaneous, independent, dull gold uncovered.
They're lost cool planets idling in the earthverse, sunless, stable, oddly preservative.

And pine mushrooms, revealed brushing humus back from a white glimpse,
whole bud exposed by fingers probing to the stalk's dull deep point, broken
from the mycelium, vast fabric of regeneration.

Earth-smell and grapple in harvesting either, soil under the nails, crouching
to get at them. I'm hungry for the lowly, humble life in them, such prizes . . .

O noble peasant, fatuous old idea! O vanity!
Mind's in the mall lots like everyone else's, mind's in the TV too many evenings

so all the hungrier for nutritive simplicity, wholeness in hand. And satiate
in the instant of discovery, no other focus nor satisfaction competing, intruding then.

Fed in fact.
Not hungry till after
in the passé meaning demeaned here, the fruitless metaphor.

***

Those flapping exuberant crows lifted
from the cedar tops in October's first serious wind
roll and swoop and fall back into foliage, playful, willing
in the air's big hands. And tonight on the roads

frogs leaping in wet joy all over the asphalt are tipped
in the balance of temperature and daylight into high-jinks
not hibernation. Tricked! They think it's spring!

Twenty-years married I'm hurrying home
to pull you towards me by the belt-loops
of your green robe, losing and gaining and losing
again in the upstart knees

-up season, a grip
on your hips, a whiff of your hair.

***

Integrity may swing on nothing
more than a lucky phrase. Most
recently: *statuesque deployment.* Coincident

with a glimpse of sunlight on trunk of cedar out my window. And I think
of the orchard, sun-strewn between the well-spaced trees. The mustering

of my powers. Oh, peril, what powers have I?
The ordered grace? The Dickinson line:

After great pain, a formal feeling comes. After happiness too, and beauty. After all.
It is the shape of afterwards in presence. A fleeting hold. Its forward-leaning voice.
Yes, and I call upon it, in its out-of-nowhere finest phrasing, its carefree

mindfulness. Let it come as I may be deserving.
Let it come anyway goddamnit! And keep coming.

These Are The Days

These are the days. They shimmer
and close (summer's finale)
against an urgency I harbour
a strenuous ache . . .

    the moon in my vise
    of window jamb and edge
    of open window, the device
    as I turn my head

of the curtain lifting
on that further background, stars
at night's extremities, exquisite, precise.
It's taken me years to get the filing right

on the chainsaw teeth to chew
straight through windfall fir. I've got it

these days out of the blue
and my chisels sharpened and oiled
in their little rack, the crowns
of the trees on the heads
of the mountains, first gold

maple flashing—an alchemy
of the leaves' breezy jiggle
and eyes' skill after all, the air
as hollow and honest as ever.

As ever and ever. Eons
of light gone cerulean ring

confirmation
in each sledge swing
on the wedge—echo, extol

the working proposition:
be home here in splendour!

Emphatic

Awaking each day in trepidation of
my work beyond the literal
or *with* the emphatic literal . . .

And which is that? Triangular stretch of exterior
wall and its window, northern end of my study
as seen from the bathroom window an expanse

of shit-brown cedar siding in horizontal
shiplap? Poetry or some lesser demon has me scanning

beyond the littoral
horizons, way past the pun

for what suddens ahead, a heartbeat each instant, emphatic

and saves the day. With work. With the work I hunger for
spoken into some thing, into feeling, and leading

me on. Oh world. Where are you?
I'm nauseous with wanting, stare hopelessly . . .

and homeless in the chest's dim cavity, vacuity,
float those toothy bits of bone, panic-triggers

I'll string to some hapless thing, innocuous
captive of the doorless eye: some aside, some siding

become this loose-ends' noose of amulet . . . but in its pitch
and sinew keeling, keening, a life-line in the squall

of meaning, in the fiction of meaning
sprawled like a sail on the sea.

Blind Corner

. . . a look down, one
heartbeat   two. Not going (wanting to!)
hooks the look in fright

back, a self-affrighting
that one *might* go, eyes off the road
careening, just staring there

into the corner under the dash. Not going in the bouncing car (no shocks).
Shock of magnetic *there* how pulling and the heavy

back meat of the skull slabbed down, one
heartbeat   two. Bouncing on the boulevard

of old trees, elms maybe, roots at cross-purposes cracking
and mounding the pavement. (Gone now. Smoothed. Widened.)

Isn't everything? Bouncing along one golden morning
in October, the magnificent trees turning. Twenty-one. And not going

sack-like near the pedals, into the pedal-well. Not naming
any of that. No world for the eye that

large-motor-muscle-surrender-ending past everything, past
involuntary response, that sapped atmosphere

we haul unlooked-for with us in the shaking body

hurtling, that lull, that dun
thumping lullaby in blind corner
curled, careening. Careless

at last! Clasped in the unsung

deep-taken. Unwrapped, flirtatious, upcast
glance at the free wheel, blur-flash past
the windscreen. And this

clangour. Clamour.

Trumpet Vine

Here was clamour and occasion.
Brash embellishment. Here at the horizon
of accomplishment trumpets nodded

abreast the green surf of foliage
about the eaves. Unfinished hang

celebratory notes, the fanfare
thread of the dark in the throat

of each bloom tugged
from the earth and under-earth
of its birth. Unfinished hangs

each muted self stepping
back from, swept
                out of its solo.

Its Jericho.
At the spot-lit core of sunlit world

a played-out hand over the heart cradles
its spilled horn, garland.
Phantom fingers twitching after

leading intricacies, intimacies of extended
melody (attachments chill and stringy)
pull closer

the duvet of November fog those mornings
light seems to push from within
the downcast leaves, their brasses
and umbers gleaming.

II

The Crowd All Over The Sign

Fifty Degrees Fahrenheit

At age five in grey light beside my tall house, our first
in North America, I was wearing a grey wool pullover.
It was fifty degrees Fahrenheit, not raining. Maybe
I'd just heard the weather forecast or maybe

that definite knowledge was somehow in me as knowledge
sometimes unaccountably is in children. I don't remember.
I remember thinking *A pullover is just right for a day like this.*

The tiny nuggets of brown glass in the grey stucco wall,
the pitted texture and exact width of the path, the three-hundred
and sixty degree dimensions of me there remain explicit, a gestalt

of detail as mysterious and atmospheric as any
course-completion in Selfhood's University. As if

I am in my parents' bedroom again learning
to tell time. The drapes are closed to help me see

the weakly, greenly glowing electric
clock-face. Is that half-past
two or half-to three? There's a point

at which perspective balks, idiomatic, then burgeons, goes fecund, a
tic in the Abstract inexplicably Life, wherein everything
is contingent, not partial, not by the numbers, not
by degrees. A whole

moment of illumination seizes
one standing in its richly furnished room forever
gaping at the carpet.

New Freeway, 1963

I remember pulling out with my dad onto the new freeway.
They had just removed the puny, embarrassed barricades and opened
its gracious curve above and adjacent to the old highway, that grind
of stop and stall and traffic-lights, businesses crowding every foot
of rubbly sidewalk. Even the newish White Spot with its upswept
airport windows and *quik serv chick'n pick'ns to your car*

gestured feebly below us, instantly out-
manoeuvred and outmoded. In a glance's
low corner a Five and Dime sign contrived
of thousands of shiny metal discs for shimmer
dimmed, aging

a generation as we shifted into high and hit
seventy as if standing still in the spacious lanes
and sparse traffic. Impossibly black

and smooth the tarmac. Impossibly silent our take-off
for the western exits, each announced and distanced
to the yard on monumental
steel in the park-

like median. Ahead, an horizon of overpass,
orange fog-lighting coming on, some leftover sky.

Owl Clover

First anecdotal evidence, and the taxidermist's
ratty specimen (an outstretched wing, the hooks
of claw-needle extended, unblinking eyes)

a wood. We make a wood of the alder bush
back of the Lions' park coming into it quiet
in the dark with school children
to call owls.

We convene a séance in a no-ghost world, listening
to the tape-deck looping aloft the hoots
and whistles of the likely species:
pygmy, barn, saw-whet, great-horned and barred.

Our mesmerizing beams criss-cross in the tree-tops.

I don't believe an owl will come. They are not
deer in headlights to be stunned into presence
by our clumsy focus . . .

Those who can hear a mouse run on packed earth
at a hundred yards, or wing at astonishing speed
through the densest cover, they must disdain
their static likenesses on earrings, brass
miniatures, Greek money . . .

our pathetic mimicry. Only the barred has spoken to me
in February fog or August starlight. I like to think he knows the pun
in his name, chooses for amusement to get me hooting. Who-who who-ooo

Who-who who-who-ooo. Who indeed? To fancy beyond
the wood, a moon, a salt-marsh meadow upland, fields
of the fodder my field guide tacks "owl" to

but doesn't explain. One panic-free, talon-less eve
for the rodent? A vegetarian moment, owlets

and elders silly as cats with catnip, rolling
and fattening like foals, in clover?
Some mollifying foolishness

in the unsheathed, soundless swoop
of disappointment, predatory sentiment
prattling after the cruel enchantment:

Well, we didn't see one but it was fun
walking around in the bush at night.
Spooky, sort of. Magical.

Parallel Parking

Tricky manoeuvre against the flow
is toughest to master. I'm out of the car at last and watching

you try it alone. Hard right, reverse
turn, pause (nose-out in imagined traffic) like rock in a river.
Hard left and back till straight, aligned. Ahead of you, invisible

in the adolescent, strident light
its pressing occasions amass now, times beyond

these practice sessions, beyond these ribboned
stakes on a rural shoulder, tentative shifts and engagement.
Times coming home to addresses as yet unknown. Sidling in at all hours across

the street from the girlfriend's. Shopping. Once just before dropping
your head on your arms on the steering wheel, the big sobs coming, oblivious
to the billowing maples in the park adjacent, the unshaken sky. Look around.

Sidewalks all slush and confetti, blown blossom and fallen leaves.
A dark past the dash-lights, stilled wipers. A door
swung open on birdsong. All your eggs
on the tarmac sizzling.

Over the empty seat you'll lean
to unlock for the passenger, a glimpse
of sword-fern, sugar-bush, weedy gravel. Further out

wheat-fields, foreign music, tundra.
White-caps. Condos. Dunes. Heavens!
The blind-spots skill and habit conjure! What a fog-up!
Big rigs and bright days flashing by. And dust. The whole of that

tutoring, testing your hesitation
at the curb of its gusting, parallel whim.

Dismantling The Treehouse

What passage is this? What elevation?
These are the tools I built with. These nails
pulled and bent are those I took up

with me, driven to enter and hold.
Flooring. Railing. And there were kids

defying gravity, their scrappy superstructure
clumsily airy, an eyrie, flamboyant.
Is this the metamorphosis

of the carpenter ant winged one
day in spring, one
in fall?

Its flung-into-air emergencies, erratic arrivals.

Or what

pulling free
of encumbrance, release
to further original purpose?

The trees. And here is my stack of used lumber.
There the salal on the path down grown back.

Moment

I had been cutting firewood, had pitched
the fir-rounds out of the bush and flipped end-
over-end the longer logs to the driveway edge, was sitting

a merciful moment where I'd worked to be, outside
thought and memory, outside the mad-mouse surge

and slump of anxiety, depression.
Inside the flat March light above

the unkempt border a bird's
flit, a chickadee, flashed
its too-quick-for-me echo

of glib and summery atmosphere insisting
there will never be more in any moment

at exactly the moment my dog not remarkable
for her sixth sense, unremarkable for sense at all, lifted

her head, got up and came to me and licked my hands
and chin and neck until I chuckled, sighed.

A Future

This is before houses.
But we have fire, a barbecue wheeled out

into a green and hummocky meadow, some lively sizzle
under the lid. Nowhere really to sit, the thick new grass
still a little wet. I am about to lift

my glass of red wine saying, hearing
already in my head, *well, old friend.* And there is wind—
a freshening, pleasing billow above near the few precarious

maples. They lean, rigid, into a far blue. Loose bark, dead boughs
unswayed, unforgiving. In the sunny air I keep looking up

in some anxiety. What out of the blue
could befall us? When we were friends
it was unthinkable we wouldn't be. What if we die

and haven't spoken? We haven't spoken as I wake.

***

Olympic tennis on TV. A medal in doubles. Canada's first, ever.
When we played in our twenties and thirties and forties you'd say,
we'll do this in our eighties. Pound played
all his life. I'd nod

but was reticent, puzzled, a bit superstitious. Who could know
how things play out? What was the far, over-reaching point?
I sensed in your insistence implicit unease, anticipatory
nostalgia, too prescient. As if you knew

and feared even then
what we'd lose: a future.

***

A future lost? It lives just round the corner as near
as memory, as contiguous

as consciousness. We live there now just
round the corner from each other. The corner there

to be turned. I know you have these moments too, of waking.
Strange intersections. The sizzle under the lid, the prescient
wine talking. A throw-back quiver in the shoulder
muscle of the perfect serve. I lift

my glass to you old friend. I say the words.

***

And then I erase your name. At the end of the day
how can I take this piece of paper
to you, with *for* _____
on the title line? I can't mail it, one more

return in the volley that wore us out. Before we were stranded
and snarled in hearsay we bored each other.
The same talk. The hollow pok/

pok of habitual affirmation. I can slip
into it now, and briefly believe, inhabit the rhythm.
But it won't pace me up your driveway eight years into

whatever life you have, whatever future. In passing
on the highway our left hands uncurl, hoist just above

our steering wheels the grudging, trusting, empty-
handed gesture of greeting

of stop

glimpsed at each other's horizons. I've built my house, keep writing.
I type in, and then erase, and then type in, and then erase, your name.

Insignificance

What is your neglect of me
to me, my voluble compeers, dumb countrymen?

Whole mountain ranges have overlooked me.
Great rivers pass me by with no glint of recognition.
Forest paths and valley roads have let me slip

through their green lenses unidentified all spring.
Past vistas. Sometimes even my wife ignores me.

But at the margins' summit, citizenship!
I have been citizen always

of Greater Insignificance, gulping
in every deaf/blind grateful face-full

of cunt or sea-air or succulent
asparagus, immensities,

the poems' first oxygen, oblivion:
your eventual reading assignment.

Hi There

Honeysuckle in its August
reprise

of May's excesses, complexities, entanglements
tosses

one unfurled bloom above the shoal of leaves along
the railing, flagging

being's bass note, base hope, dauntless
singularity

as attached and flighty and flaring forth
as the brash accost my daughter has been hissing

at me most of this, her fifteenth year. Hands up
framing a grimace her fingers curl half-
fisted, claws flexed in warning

play. Challenge. Fierce
inarticulate greeting: *BUH KEEEE!*

Stationery Almond

A sheet of creamy vellum in hand and waved
idly making a point before filing opens surprising

depth of field towards the walls. That's the colour
for them! That's the light we'll live in, the welcoming

hue through the windows we'll splash
our dreams and shadows across for years, cast

our future towards. Nutty gesture gets us there best

as usual, is a singular treat perched
high on the topping, a butter-crunch
succulent on the tongue past trifle

into sustenance, as rich and abiding
a nip of serendipity as abode might be
bounty of shelter and expression's atmosphere.

A Kiss Beneath Wisteria

Amidst heavy bloom, a mauve
abundance, next to bees, head in the clouds
of heady fragrance my eyes close in that swoon

every love scene features
so true it risks (and is)
cliché each reckless
time anticipating

your lips brushing mine.
That doesn't happen, happens

there only, imagined
barefoot on the patio
beneath wisteria.
The world past the curtain

of blossom is this one, open-
ended as the page but ending

somewhere
before you kiss me.

Pineapple Weed

Between absence and presence, between
leaving and return falls the shadow (caress,

impasse) of down-thrust rigid wings in once-
over, in a stiff-fingered grope onto
Sea Island, copping a feel of the bulging shade
trees and homey older houses of Burkeville, of the freeways

and bridges and of the Airport Viewing Park, smudged into the tremor
and stir of his anticipation in the last hour awaiting
her homecoming. Even the clouds have caught

his turbulent mood, teasing clouds in late sun and breeze flashing
their fresh underwear and imperious dark looks and look he has finally

got down on the ground, his red windbreaker a flung marker there
beside the memorial park bench, between the asphalt paths mapping the actual

runways across the rough lawn. He has got so close stretched out
on his stomach he recognizes the cracked clay and inconspicuous
weeds from a childhood on the prairies. Great planes

are one by one catapulting into the west with a skidding quickly-
corrected little swerve in the thunder and heat wave and haze
of exhaust as each revs up and releases
its brakes. At Departures

a couple is touching too fondly and insistently, the fantail
of distance aflutter already in their display . . . (A stunted self-heal

those plants might be, or minute, primordial
chamomile. He'll ask her about them when she comes

down from the jet-lag. They'll look in books.) At Arrivals
a couple is melded together as if to go on thus in utter
oneness were inevitable. Over all of this

rushes the shadow of the rigid wings, dashed and pebbly and flecking on the sea's
wrinkled sheen, on the textured earth, on the houses and details and yearning.
Then suddenly slowed and weighty, freighted, it pulls and squeezes its maker
to itself until it seems as nothing come

to huddle under the stopped machine, a still thing except as the sun moves,
as pedestrian as our human shadows, compressed

beneath and between us as if comprehended, as if run to ground.

The Cave In The Coals

Would you enter this luminous centre? I had a friend
who wanted to put his face in the fire. And everyone gathers

around a woodstove in a kitchen. *Such a penetrating
heat*, they say. And the origin both of community

and contemplative solitude—the opportunity staring
through flame's window, through that door of tempered glass

into that intensity, to speak without looking
around. To overhear

oneself. To muse aloud, obliquely
universal. This was the centre

for millennia until television. I thought then of my friend's desire,
It is despair of being heard or known. Or a fiendish, sudden appetite

for rage and pain made manifest, explicit.
Or the profoundest hope of the handsome

for disfigurement. To face the world and others turned
away, a liberating roominess. Gazing

into fire's old face today I see for the first time
an emberred hollow near the draught, incandescent space

on the underside of an alder log beckoning. *Shelter,*
it promises past the rim of flame. Like the promise

of a woman's body. Depths of heat and pleasure
and then, as hearth in earth ends, and heart in art, eschewing
their initial heroics, regaining their cool, each

exhausted half-husk rolls
onto its side, a geode opened

earth egg on my study's sill. After the puff of gas or dust or tiny gasp
of vacuum broken into the saw bisected stone

for its treasure of absence—cup
of encrusted immaculate shatter, crystalline, sparkling

firmament of puckered O past slippery
bright lip, past buff and bluff and buffeting
where anything one is might hold, where everything

one might be grows. Where we, oh human family, breathe
in, breathe out, keep company.

Arrangements

Rubble of shells
and sticks and pebbles at tide-line
kids assembled and abandoned

called home . . .   Its value
can't be told, old selves, remembered
friends, though re-reading you, hearing you through

an evening of Debussy duets
and harmonies from The Gondoliers
syncopates debris, proposes a new prismatic

care for what we could do. Can do!
Our notes resurrect summer light. Keening

through the windows, against the logs
aligned on the beaches for orderly
sunbathing, against the flushed

expectant sea, flash droll convivialities . . .
This late sun strikes wide of us, past me. Plumb
as I will our suspended depths and brilliancies

detail is preponderant, magnificent
wash and splash of specifics, essential
digressions—among the budding fuchsias, into

forgotten upper corners
of our living rooms, across
the mouths of wine glasses . . .

Sensational, senseless light.
Go with your cameras and try.
Go with your verses, your best brochures.

It's sad down the alleys. Crows squabble
near the sky, shit unabashed on the sundecks.
Blackberry vines find lawns to terrorize.
Things lose sight of their lengthening

shadows, affinities, their maidens
clinging

singing goodbye.

The Crowd All Over The Sign

These are my loves and significant
others come up from the city, come

down out of the hills. In mind of the deranged
coyote, too near the campsite mid-afternoon. In cross-trainers, view-
finders. In dusty sandals, dumb hats, swim-suits. Assembled. We are at the gate.

Dressed for summer, summer
becomes us, a penetrant dry heat hugging
the cottons, the dark varnish. On the breeze

pine resin, whiff of reed (no whiff of reading), cloud fluff, sulphur
of the black Honda just gone by. Splinters of shadow in the horizontal grain

across the deep-routed place name. And us all over it. A little in the way
of the white lettering, the blue neutrality

on high. We've got hold of the huge chipmunk
hewn from a single tree, the tree-tops behind us as if sprung

from our heads turned aside a little, out of the sun.
Not merely substantial. Something superlative, extra-

terrestrial leaned on the blonde stone foundation, the glare, this end
of that unlikely far-off sparkle, that fervent hint

of lake's deep equilibrium.

Large Mirrors

Large mirrors in the tall cool rooms and spaces
of antique, gracious houses are insightful . . . They gaze

wall-eyed past grooming and improvement unafraid
at worn veneers and shadows, were placed
on a landing of the grand staircase for the glances

in passing of those satisfied at last with glimpses
of an oaken atmosphere uninhabited, full
of itself. They are easy with either

eventuality in a dining room festive or forlorn. A floral
centrepiece, the chandelier, rising laughter, the risen
speech-maker, enchant them equally. Some day

you'll show up early, over-dressed, self-conscious,
or under-dressed, too nonchalant.

Or you'll peek in just for fun, mid-
morning, suddenly hungry. Despite the drawn curtains

they will see you coming.
Someone might shout, *surprise*! Or whisper something.
There will be the honest light, reflection, nothing more.

Far-fetched

Till feeling prove a reciprocal
physics, a common quantum,
we know the earth doesn't love us.
But such a profusion of roses 'round the door

cascading, we rush to exclaim *a hundred, a hundred
and fifty?* White roses. How many in the drowse
of the thousands of words for them humming

in the subtext of a summer morning
engulf and elude us? Who knows

but that the numberless (notorious
sand-grains, atoms, stars . . .)

bloom in their swirling eddies and channels
to rapturous illustration everywhere. Cast-off
from counting, sounding, they tide unknowably wide

of the mind's arc in the dark immensities, petals
strewn on its sundeck as far-flung, far-

fetched (and as fetching)
as affection. What next
to affection do we know so hugely

lovely and preposterous, so
incautiously excessive, selfless?

III

Idiot Of Place

Depleted Geranium

So long coming to the call
of the misheard, long trek under the quick smile flutter
of pleasure, the flag of the mischievous phrase, to the actual cold-

frame, to the rust-coloured stalk in its lace of mould
and leaves like flakes of rust adhered
or fallen. Here it sings

in the flight it knew of pineapple or rose
scent rising through fingers

ruffling its top-most foliage in the casual, loving
way they might ruffle the hair of a knee-high child.
Only last summer. Only last

summer. Too much to ask. Good-bye coming
to the call of the misheard like a homeless
hound, desperate in the half-hope

of any name you choose, half-
starved in half-light. Glow, geranium.
You are no rusted scrap of iron, no flaky axiom.

You are the armour-piercing shell.

You are a geranium, vivid and vital
as lucky accident, tenacious

as lingering illness. You are
the ears' warm oil, their laurel crown (true

grail to sounding's errant knight, an *arriviste's*
next step on scale) your place replete

as any in the long coming-to
we live through, live through, live through . . .

Labyrinthitis

. . . a condition of the inner ear, possibly viral, characterized by vertigo, nausea, and sometimes, as a consequence of those symptoms, agoraphobia, panic . . .

You Are Here

Yes, you are. Blood-
red dot or white star
marks your predetermined spot

amidst the hurrying strangers, shoppers.
At the nexus of marble avenues, escalators,
under the rotunda, next to the lottery kiosk,

we planned for this.
(The muzak, the legend, everything . . .)
We planned

for your arrival or return
like a lost child, found money.
Your bewildered standing here,
locating yourself, re-evaluating, seeking

direction—all this we anticipated.
We put it under amber glass
where you could go, or be

and here you are. Welcome.
Welcome. Au revoir.

Lab Y

The bull-headed boy
won't take his meds
till every thread
tugs back to

Who am I? Why me?
where she made offer
of the yarn ravelled under
her skirt and hid

the embalmer's sword
at the mouth forever, at the gates
of the last word. Monster, victim, saviour cleave

and clone in penultimate home, this room
at the end of the hall

whose West door makes its little sucking
seal upon closing, disclosing

perfect lighting, perfect dark
in the jar.

Spires

Tho' spires aspire and a leaping sun
glance off the glaciers and gilded cupolas
dancing its frantic hallelujahs

the only roof to life is death. Shadows
slipped indoors behind the kids
raiding the fridge

will be fed. Decline and disintegration
come ahead. Reclining I'm already lifted

from my bed and sped obliquely
spaceward on a regular basis. My head

spazzes left   as if something

wants attention. So swizzle
me good in your shaker. Nibble my olive
asplash above the promontories. Fire up

the rotisserie. There wherever
light lies, scattering, shaft me.

Mays

too many to remember drift
downstream on lovers' dreaming
lain in stupendous poppies, surf

of periwinkle at the bed's prow
and in their wake unbraiding

in their fixed stare
eddies where the gazing goes.

Amaze

Central sense resides intact, miraculous
within the tinnitus. The tinny voice, *you*

can hear me can't you? persistent
as a stylus slipped

into its groove, its grove, grates
and grovels for the long notes, the one way

inevitable, inevitably gnawing
to the record's core. *Do you listen*

like this? Amazing Grace lifts . . .
But the speaker is . . .

The speaker sits
in a slowed whirl, whorls

imprinted in sun-swirl, in snail-
shell, in cedar burl. Its emblem.

Maize

Each newborn Hopi gets a perfect ear
of corn, and then on the lip

of the mesa, the sun's kiss, his name, niblet
in the gut-brain of the world

nugget and whole note of the now-
mapped DNA, piecemeal, peaceable

laddered and spiralled
downscale.

Lost Lake

On a drive to cool off in summer gloaming
(the kids clamouring since morning for a swim)
our hard turn at the first intriguing sign, *Lost
Lake*, is the first of nine in a mile

of gravel
narrowing
up into

darkening reaches of mountain shadow:
forest to one side, precipice

on the other. The second sign
in a glimpse of headlights: *Danger.
Logging Trucks. No Public Access.*

No pullouts, no shoulder. To turn around
in the gullet of a switchback could take
minutes, six moves

of the family wagon angled
across the whole road
in the full dark

leaning on the horn.

Cul-de-sac

Down ears' well on
eyes' leash fondled
up the ganglia sniffed
and tasted, briny

all gathers encoded
in brain fold, soul's
appendix. Now

is father of the next
instant the whole distance.
There is only one

opening in this life. Chemo-

electric trace translated
ripens the farther, anxious
fester of the binaries. Its pleasure

clasped in soft-lipped
pouches knows

simpatico a treasure
deep in the vowels.

The Simple Life

No bestial whiff discernible
in disinfected air, the blood scrubbed
from the corridor, the roof flown

on its buttresses, the structure itself
dismantled and its stones set out
as New Age maze in meadows, malls

for a quest-becalmed ambling
between them, an enigma danced, still

there is no simple life. It's best
to husband some complexity

one's not thrust into, charm
its writhing efflorescence, its statuesque
deportment. Wheedle, taunt

and worry it. It will yield
exactly this: *veronicas*

as if beyond it utterly, drenched
in sunlight, talking to yourself
or someone who left

you alone returning
to drive downtown for a doughnut.

Vast Vaults

of blue
and white flash off the sea

Touring Utah: An Object Lesson

Tease (from the van's speed, mind's
slip-stream, the shif-

ty vistas) landform, fossil of a cloud.
Going where you think to
go: Four Corners, Inspiration Point,

Angel's Landing. Work 'round the case
of the Anasazi displayed in shreds
of sandal, 800 AD corn-on-the-cob.

Buy turquoise tumbled by the Navajo
and an arrowhead recycled as a charm

against the wind's slick way with it, them, you

(old earth entire on its lathe)
throwback, smooth-talker.

Can you ease down the sliprock, toes
to the river's exhaustive marginalia

and not know?
Pant up the trail

and to hand in the canyon
sandstone in flesh-tones
is hot for you.

The Chiropractor's String

Before the practitioner's touch, the jaunty ski-jumps
of her knuckles off your vertebrae and her blind, conscientious
probing within you, you must back up, barefoot

to the abstract, to the notion of pure verticality, visibility.
Though the spine on the wall-chart sports an organic
curvature, the string's measure is more exacting, more

like the flight of the soul or the fall of angels. Like light
in its direct descendancy. More trued-up beam than bearing

column for the creature you are, crawling in, in spasm.
Soon she is rolling your head in her hands for the snapping

assertion, the series of clicks that proclaim alignment.
But the string strict on its pedestal won't sing assent

to your prone, though improved, condition. It's the tweaked nerve
of your body's nooks and knots, the tight wire of the *chakras*.
It is the pitiless harp of perfection, and twangs

all by itself in the corner.
Or it is bodiless, mindless snippet
plunged plumb from its hook at the height of a man

to the floor with nothing of footing nor standing nor dreaming
to live in, to embolden as we must, nothing to muscle into upward being.
Icon of heavy chrome and floss, clinical window-dressing, apprenticing

hat-rack, it loiters near the doorway like a senile butler, absurdly
grave. You will somehow rise and walk

past it to receive the benediction and deduction dictum
of the Health Care Plan, and the New Age brochure
and herbal sample free upon exit.

Stand: Wildwood BC

The blush of red alder catkin
that is our coastal spring's first rose

smudges the lake edge below a stand of fir
on upland slope in a slant of sun.

Here we are well past the barricades.
Here we have come forward

to the land in the span of a life, the span
of a hand and mind turned to true work.

In resonant example you can stand, unbending
as if from limbing a felled, well-chosen specimen

and inhabit its new stretch of space and timber
in both directions, both dimensions. Stand

beside the cooling saw and feel the breeze,
the dappled light's complex beneficence

upon you, a teasing bounty. Here in the dignity
of husbandry stand not *against,* not *for*

but *with* what the earth roots and raises. Be more
than harvester. At home in your wild humanity be

harvested, the human grain of the wood.
Its mindful belly-full, deep denizen. Its being.

Idiot of Place

At fifteen on a green like this I paced
and stood, raising

the bow at the various ranges, losing
heart in the arcs of the arrows falling
short, placed

third in a field of four. Distracted
and inconsistent in first, exacting instances,

I've apprenticed since as artisan
of the oblique trajectory, the nominally

bleaker prospect. There is no human spirit not
at a loss in the world, not smaller

than the flit of silver on cottonwood leaf
as breeze and a brightening day choose

to have me see at fifty-three the slumped
plots and tilted markers at the margins

under the trees where we are released to our limits
in the labouring drone of mower and backhoe

and croon of the golden oldies through somnolent afternoon.
Unfashionable tune and tarnish, diminished

expanses, compel my searching glances to any
momentary shine, glint in the mossy lines or tiny flag

of flame from the refinery burn-off chimney beyond
a leafy horizon. In reaches above

bough-weave and tipped stones'
obliterated script, a summer cloud mass tumbles

into name and doom. Into nothing
but this bronze work to do.

Twinned Towers

Hagia Sophia

Deep in the cities fabulous and real
we've fled from, sailed to (and inhabit still
in intricate streets and dreams and histories
of difficult accommodation)

mosaics of craft and statecraft shimmer . . .
minarets embellish a Christian dome . . .
the Salonicians live as secret Jews . . .

At checkpoint and convention centre,
at bank machine and communal well,
alloys of hope and fear hard-minted
in elaborate Jerusalems, uneasy truces

are currencies extruded now to promissory settlement
and fierce, obtuse, far-flung antagonisms: cave complexes bristling
with Kalashnikovs, skyscraper missiles of the money markets yearning

heavenwards. New words for heaven scrabble
at the air, pillow on the airwaves, balloon,
absurd, oblivious to consequence as if
earth itself and all our fine built world

were *their* abstraction, a footnote
in the mad cosmologies, a miss-step
from oblivions of wealth or martyrdom.

Major Arcanum

And from that miasma, from clear (ironic) sky, veers
spectacle so explicit, so sheered across meaning, it beggars
rhetoric—begs parallel, begs parable, begs

blind word take its measure, its flash of fire and fall
to mind. Where we are each that everyman

of forsaken downtown streets. Dazed he loiters
with his shopping-cart load of beer cans and worthless bundles,
loiters in his greatcoat cinched with twine, mumbling in the glow

of row upon stacked row of TVs endlessly transmitting
the same image. We are that man and his extended
family in the desperate Afghan villages, everyone
crowded around the one TV endlessly transmitting

the same image. And we are those forever at ground zero, flesh
in the rubble, the New York rescuers under the floodlights,
the Taliban gravediggers eager in white in no-man's land
near Mazar-e sharif to retrieve

the bodies, to become the bodies
abandoned to Allah, the dross of the dream. Ours is the foot

in the door of the deep secret, the ultimate empire, Emptiness
where each life soldiers and flounders
to learn its meaning . . .

Babel

     . . . the porn channel playing
72 Virgins all night long, Wall Street's biggest
discounts, the mall's best deal: 100% Down and
Don't Pay Till Eternity. This is fate's chance, clockwork
cell-phone serendip, the box-

cutter undetected in the shoe, the one-off one-way thru the numbers
game of miscounted, countless dead, the 9-11 ouija dial-up—perennial

emergency. "Everything's changed," the same
bush-league gurus are screaming. "Muhammed
al akbar!" "Don't stop shopping!"

Canadian National

Dear neighbours, friends: As always, our thoughts are with you.
We have shared your shock, your terror. But now the thousands of travellers

delayed here, whom we sheltered in our homes,

have safely arrived in your airports. The shadowy Arabs we harbour
have proved innocuous. The powders in the envelopes, sawdust and off-

cut of empire folded (as ever since Cold War into hinter-
land, buffer zone, void between warning and target) have been shaken down
and out. Into nothing. Nothing happens here.

You know that. You watch 60 Minutes and never see it
happen. See it never happen. Come home again to your second
home, to the provinces, to the world's tallest

free-standing structure. The restaurant on top revolves
beyond the spin of influence. We have simulator rides,
a double-value dollar, mountains

of gift shop teddy-bears done up in scarlet
leaves and tunics, cuddly for your company, eager

to live out their days on day-beds in Florida. You will be safe here.
No purposeful fanatic could pursue you, would pilot the oblique intent towards

irrelevance to do us harm. And look, an expanse
of city beneath us that looks like a city
of yours. Come stand

on the glass floor, and peering, feel
the world at your feet as far as Niagara
Falls in the distance. In the further distance,
Rochester. (N.Y.!) (but only Rochester . . .)

Crane

Growl and rumble in the skyline's hole
in flat light over the Hudson
of a world on hold, in waiting . . .

Not for survivors in their imminent tombs.
Not for the shamming Imam in his mountain.
Not for the CEO on his smug plush. (Not shovel
nor smart bomb nor markets collapsing can flush them . . .)

but for the rest of us

trapped in the dark of our devolution, in the dark
rain and stutter of the bombs on the other
side of the world, in the inarticulate
annihilation, retribution—for us

this heavy lifting, trucking, kneel and bow
of the earth-mover, shape-shifter, spirit
of the mass, and the derricks' swinging benediction above

the work's ascent by an anchored increment, just clear
of the girdered rubble. These durable materialists

(true fundamentalists)
are reaching for us in the subterrain, the unseen

where invisible trains link in their tunnels
and ground water presses the dry-socket membranes
and millions of conversations sprint in the micro-filaments.
Where the gold is hidden, where the 18th century anchor unearthed
for the towers' first foundation (at loose ends
in dry-dock three decades in the basement)
is newly burdened, embedded again

in more than bombast and stale air . . .
in ballast beneath our delusions
they grapple and winch and pray for us, our trusted
machines, our first-born prehensile mentalities.

Dioce

To the lost self caged in desolation, in rigid weld, to the razed
and levelled imagination under the mesh (in contra-
puntal reverie) spring glimpses

of the cloud cities, that tall exquisite filigree
of bridgework, the jewelled stair

to *Dioce, whose terraces are the colour of stars* . . .
On the high wires, braving the stresses *to trace
the visionary company of love, its voice
an instant in the wind,* sings.

(Too far to follow far, too will-o'-the-whisper preposterous
before the brazen empty chair at breakfast, the blinds opened
on the unchanged street, the relentless drumbeat of the last phrase
of phone-call before the fall from airspace . . .

I love you in wrenching reverberation) but that singing might be, is, oh
be enough to tease us a moment from the small screen and hard
reflection in plate-glass, from the dark facades, shards

and declensions of grief. It *is* enough to send us unclenched, strolling
free a moment in the sweet city, the city saved, a book in hand or a lover
on one's arm again, alive in the soft air and

at home a moment leaning on that big stone or plane tree or damp grass
in the park, or pulling open the dear weight of the great doors
by their hand-worn handles of honey-toned brass . . .

It was in a cage near Pisa, Ezra
Pound found and sang that famous phrase of his famous canto, one line, one
mention of his heavenly city, *Dioce*, and at the farthest reach, I fancy, of the shadow
of that famous tower . . . As if of some god's sundial, impossibly extended
the shadow-finger that touched him then, that touches everyone poised

in grief asking (at last) nothing . . . As Crane at a loss alone in Brooklyn
encountered aloft the visionary company, and Yeats

in his grey fortress of old age
dreamed dazzling Byzantium.

Mt. Daniel

Those TV dead are not my dead. But I have dead
and loved ones alive to fear for, and loss to fear,
as we all do, knowing what's coming—

Armageddon, or not. I have that compassion-anxiety
easiest to carry in the dark days before Christmas
bringing in firewood, or climbing Mt. Daniel.

It's a local hill, or hills really, soft forested mounds
on the torso of the peninsula, a motherly bosom

but a hard hike nevertheless (up creek-bed and slippery edge)
I take with my wife and oldest son, joking and talking

as we catch our breath, pushing into what I've always known
and can't know of relentless ascent, disappearing
centre. The soul's sad enterprise.

If you're reading this you too
are moving away from ground zero. Time takes us, grit
in our eyes and shattered glass underfoot perhaps, or flushed for now

with righteous fury—or thoughtful, troubled, puzzling
it out. Lucky trajectory, luckless orbit, a foetal doubled-
over anguish, a grateful sigh—whatever its gesture
you'll know what I mean when I say

it's a measure of who we are, this movement (mine
conversational, cautiously inclusive, Canadian) a measure
of our reach (always incomplete) toward each other, and of our retreat

from the self-obliterating centres of power, the black holes.
It's a measured response we make—
personal, merciful, a little

lonely—a re-determination
of the world in its details, its scale, its inevitably
unjust distinctions. Between the peaks of Mt. Daniel

in mossy clearings we come upon ragged circles
of placed stones, moon-rings the native girls construct
in their night on the mountain, in their sea-change

into womanhood. And down-slope over
the precipices, glimpses of Oyster Bay through mist, a bend
in the highway, someone's boat

pulled out for the winter. I think of Hart Crane's
beautiful word, *curveship,* and the delicate

tonnage of counterbalance engineers have accomplished
under Pisa's leaning tower, to keep it standing. How partial
all this is. No straight lines in art or nature. No perfect circle. No finish.
But shades of resemblance, remembrance. If not resolution, the long spin

in our deepest thinking of gyre, helix, the messy swirls
of galaxies as they swing back in

toward still-point, starburst, ends loose at best
to some shared influence . . . a magnetic, compelling shagginess
to the back-lit old-growth where the trail winds down.

Gound Zero

Sleight of mind, peripheral
flicker and glitch, where consciousness catches

a cuff on the candelabrum, flapping sight
of itself alight. A flashing

zebra underneath. You name it.
O skeletal mimic. O scaffolding.
Say anywhere. Say the boarding-

house reach, believer. In elegant dark.
In dark without contradiction or nuance.

So far, far from your feet on the floor-plan. A towering.
A toppling. And all that rubble of facility.

It will have to be home. It will have to be right here
again. The icy stair. The cat-shit on the handrail. Cloudy sits there

all night. In the morning I light the fire and let her in
and take the little shovel for the hearth and scoop the shit

messily off into the leafless, tangled (I've forgotten the name it being
mid-winter . . . blooms in June, is sensationally fragrant, creamy
and vermilion . . .) vine.

I'm terrible with names. The world is terrible with names.
And worse without? Not jasmine. Not clematis. Not even

close. I have it in poems, could find it somehow.
It'll come to me when I walk away.

Airing The Bed

Laundry Day

That we in our days might be the lift
and billow of Egyptian cotton drying in sunlight
we'll jockey the nightmares through their soggy ovals
to exhaustion, to the flashbulb/champagne finish. We can

get here from there, yolk of dawn on the sills, surrendering
with grace to somnolent comfort, the easy warmth. It's time . . .

And forgive us our wrinkles, as we are relentless somnambulists also
in habit's ether, second-nature

shaking out the duvet, pulling and tucking the fitted
sheet smooth, fluffing the pillows . . . The intimate creases
our bodies knew darkly have been twice shown

the ceiling and gone over lightly, by hand,
their secret scents and snug stains sung *al fresco*, each
dreamy conundrum and embrace relaxed and released towards landscape.

Unwinding Sheet

                                         And everywhere the dead
must be rousted and rolled out! What use are they, slouched

in attitudes of slumber? There are histories
to be brought to life and the dreary

memorial drone to be interrupted, crossover-rock and zephyrs
gate-crashing the crypt. There is regret and grief and grievance

to be harvested, threshed and baked into pretzels. Pressure-
wash the ossuary boxes! Empty the urns! Hurry the ashes
to meadow and ocean, fondling and waving

the grey lives goodbye. Earth, relieved
of the weight of the lain-low will spin
a tick quicker, spring
for the beer and then the coffee, keeping it up
all morning, breezy and wakeful as a new

star, a flirtatious aspen. The sad songs
will be maudlin only, and the tragedies
bemused adventure.

Airs

Rockabilly this afternoon, then maybe a little opera. Muted
blues in the candlelight later. Of course we will lie down again.
But never forever! (Let us pray.) Grant us each day

a spirited resurrection. Deliver unto us the immense

vocabularies of sentience, and the hum-along lyric sheet. We'll be putting on
airs I can tell you. We'll be deep-breathing. I'm wearing the pewter

paper-weight in the shape of a sand-dollar
over my heart. And the silver frog. Whatever brambles

are stuck to my jeans. Enamel every cell and syllable
of our restless aubade, our raucous *Te Deum*. Bejewel and bedevil us

with appetite and empty shell . . .
and buff us benightedly, blessedly
trivial

into thin air in our sleep.

Hallowell

Because what's close and obvious is most
elusive, and what's next-door's most easily

ignored, or disappears in doorless mist
I've been walking, walking, walking

to discover the mountain I live on. I push through alder-brush and up
the hydro-cut like a tick in dog's fur, hungry for nutrient, elevation.
Top of the head or behind the ears. Then digging in. Ribbons

of waterfall dangle above me, glimpses of aqua sky at sky-line
through the nation's oldest trees. The yellow cedars rooted there
before Christ thrive still in the wet alpine, no forest fire for two thousand years.

Ravens sweep over, a silent quartet, each
a corner of flexing quadrangle, one tumbling.

My walking-stick swings forward from my left hand and touches
earth every three and a half paces. (Hey Gurdjieff! Thanks for the right-
brain crowbar!) There's elk-shit on the trail, grouse surprised into clumsy

flapping, heavenly mirror of lakes below
and apace a counting verse, an omen verse, using crows: *Three
is a wedding, four is a birth* . . . this mountain, my thinking, a blind hunch
into cloudscape, an untried dimension . . .

Widest gesture slips wide of its depth

of field at dinner in my friend's left hand thrust up to be
the nest of the secretive murrulet in old-growth, his right thrust
down the foggy distance of its pre-dawn flit into unawakened sea

for the sand lance, a sliver-flash of food. He hangs there a moment aloft, brightly
grinning, attentive, like a kid playing airplane steeply banking, stalling, hearing
something . . . the whistling extremities, potentialities, windy engines . . .

***

Because remotest glints snap into line—web, shine
and mob language, and mind's all scud and spindrift at cliff
and corners on the downcoast drive . . . palpitations, surges, uncanny
and unnerving slip-knots of tie-down, splashy gestalts

or only the tide-flats left behind . . .

I stay in bed all morning burrowed
into the muffle and dusk of my need
to inhabit the mountain I live on—to fathom
and deepen its holy well of fortuitous naming. I dip again into

the half-way lake, tea-coloured, boggy, deep-mossed to every edge
where my son and I swam last summer. There I lose sight again
of my body treading water. I stand again on my roof-deck
as on a summer morning early in the drama
of the mountain's shadow

retreating, sun-slick edging up to me over the long ridge
of summit, across the cedar planking. Were we Coast Salish
I'd take off my Swaihwé face and pass the bug-eyed mask to you
as slabs and planes of glassy basalt, edgy

and interior but outside spatial relationship lean

near me in fragments, chunks
of cross-section. Foreign. What's lit them up
deep as we suddenly are in the granite? A featureless black

at the back of the head feels fuller, accurate.
And a coppery glow

from immensity's centre, the heart of mass, from the mouth
of the shaft of abandoned copper-mine I'll climb to one day

is accomplishing verdigris
in vertigo over the tailings, blue-
green oxidation in the world of light.

Everest

Traverse

Ready? (Ever?) Wanna take a run at it?
Got your retread crampons handy and your five-
year-old soul? May 1953, Hillary

conquered Everest. And I set foot in Canada.
Who was that boy on a boat, boy on a train?
There he descends the gracious stair of the S.S. Atlantic's

Italianate dining room. There he keeps down his breaded
cutlet for twenty minutes. The cavernous railway station lounge
in Quebec City takes him briefly in, echoing. Nothing of the broad
ocean nor the bald prairies enters

his little rooms of memory, his first way-stations in the New World.
The heavy canvas curtains of the upper berth, their fastenings, fascinate.
Who foresees them anyway, the outdoor earthly high-wire
possibilities? A walkabout moon hung

sixteen years in the future, and further out
unfathomed deep blue sea. In the wings already is that the wan
archaic irony, going there? The whiff of re-runs? Oil boom, oil boom,
oil boom. Perchance foreshadowy post-modern gloom sought even

Calgary, where uncle waited in his grey Chevy. The towering cumulus began
to accumulate detail, interpretation, not meaning, accumulate mockery

in dissolving peaks, shifty definitions, ponderous determined foot-
prints leading across the snow bridge over the crevasse under the cornice.

Off Centre

My first ascents are first of all asides, accidental, passing once
under lilac on the walk to piano lessons so that I've never forgotten
its fragrance, its mauve. Or the time-warp off-white shade of sky

that summer afternoon I took a notion
to go downtown, telling no-one,
and ventured through the neon noose

of lariat encircling the ticket booth and revolving doors of the Corral
cinema to reappear never missed on 32nd avenue north-west just
in time for dinner, a miracle

of filmic, existential magic. Dashing one winter rush-hour dusk across
Centre Street dodging headlights I was brought up
short, shaken

on the slush mound of median in the skid on the horn
of the driver's scream, *Do you want to get
yourself killed!?*

Icefall

Norgay stretching a handkerchief of Union Jack into
summitry's fierce wind leans upon the immense

logistics of accomplishment, the busy purposes.
Before I had a dozen books I'd put labels on the edges
of the shelves, crayoned categories, helpless not to. And worst
of all, knew better—grumpy and disappointed, pursued even so that wasteful

craziness. On task. Countless false starts into the blur. *South
With Scott, Journey To The Centre Of The Earth*. Tarzan and Lone
Ranger gone on ahead tuned up my thin air orchestras. I played my heart out
in the backyard, hallucinated side-kicks at my side, loyal Tontos, Janes. All went

sideways. Only new footfall
of isolate daydream broke

the crust—oases drifted over in my wake, scatter-shot
bead on the big heroics. Unstrung lineage, no lifeline, no ice axe, no

training to speak of, no speaking in the monsoon howl but plaintive secret hymn
to myself and a smoking Daisy air-gun banging at blank air. Avalanche

control? Avalanche warning?

Mid-stride

                    . . . *because it's there*
(George Mallory, lost near the summit, 1924)
Because it's there

then not. Gone underfoot or over
snow-skim into atmosphere. Since Hillary 1200
summiteers. 175 deaths against the tallest question, what

to do with a life? Not secondarily (schools
for Sherpas) but in morning glare off
the glacier. On the trail today I sing
the chant of the quick glance

down. Under the scissors of limb-shadow
monk's tonsure of small boulder exposed with its fringe
of new grass casts up to me a blonde, flesh-like
regard, weak sunlight

of re-opened fontanelle in standing burial, in packed earth stymied.
As I would be on those ledges (you've seen them, thousands
of feet of sheer above and sheer below the miniscule

encampment) suspended mid-stride in meander chanting *Bow
and Elbow, bear scat, scuff sign,* mulling over the milling elk
tracks, any diverting and gentler surprise. Any diverting
and gentler purpose persisted in dumbs

down the mountain, home. Ground water trickles from severed
old root in a cut bank. Reversal, refreshment. And over there, wild
violets. Prayer flag. Prayer wheel. How ever to unpack a next

step, then another . . . How (everer) to walk the earth?

Horizon

Like a streak of morning under overcast,
the wordless under the word, little curve

of earth's surface one covers even going
to the compost bin, even mowing the lawn.

Unknown, unknown but for cadence in us, a pace
participant in permanence, a vibrancy, pulse
not dramatic, not abstract either, of eternal

presences, of everywhere. A steady
light. Where gods move to accomplish
the pointedly pointless, deeply impossible thing.

The Sermon on the Mount

Be ye therefore perfect, even as your Father
which is in heaven is perfect.
                        —Matthew 5:48

The prophet came this way. Must have.
In pyjamas maybe on a June morning, a Sunday.

The men and women, friends and family,
slept on in the cool house in their temple
of talk past midnight in the press

of ideas and ideals against each other
and into their pillows. From the wine-glass littered rooms

and along the orchard's edge, over the sluices
and up through toadflax into sage brush and rabbit brush
came the prophet, head full of what to say, and

where to say it—came not so far as the slope where the name of the town
was spelled out in quartzite capitals, not so far as the one ponderosa pine
near the first peak, not so far as the eastern precipice. But far enough.
Below, the lake paid rapt attention to the sky. The prophet gathered

everything in wide embrace: multitudes
of bunch grass, cherry leaf, quail and chicks in deep
shade under the trees. Tremors of light and breeze and water

performed their sun-up miracles. But only the words she had rehearsed
entranced her. Only imagining the grown-ups hanging
upon them. Only those heady, propelling words

unsummoned by the breathless world refused to come
all the way there and be spoken. In sudden awe
of unconsidered immensities, or at the whim

of wilful thought exhausted, wind-
shifted, unconsciously practical (as one avoids
scat on a path) she stepped aside

and over where everything slips
against knowing, eases past and pushes
in a new heat and shimmer of essence towards this, us.

IV

Wind Chime

Sundeck in Houselight

Holy and goofy from under the eaves' brow, from under
the drooping eyelid of the blinds, out of season, conciliatory
a vague light falls, interior light gone out past its purpose

to make a little floor, smudged at the edges, on the cedar planking.
There the plant pots have been pulled to the wall, the railings have nothing
to hold but leafless vine, no-one to hold back. There might be mist, a condensed

attention, hovering. What is this world to the world, compelling pause

in memory as if before some icon of belief? A door?
One of those precise, bright cubes

excavated in the chests of saints, wherein their shimmery vermilion hearts
float, crowned

in a white intensity, in light from nowhere? Were the gods here
dancing? We lay

in those deck-chairs folded and hung on the wall, well-oiled and sacrificial once
in direct sunlight, who haunt the huge surround now (the floorless murk
unbuilt, unmanifest) or from within, from the dining-room window

pursue enigma in the twice-tried, tireless, observable spaces.

Inheritance

Whose sun-in chartreuse is this, incandescent
in April's mosses, maples? Older than gods, as old

as the earth it is fatherless, motherless. Older
than human suffering it's as urgent, as pressing

as the most recent anti-war
e-mail petition. A steady insistence

informs it, an inexhaustible energy, a magnetic succulence

inedible, asexual, alchemical, inherited
without entitlement. Without entitlement it will age

to no-one's flatter green imperceptibly
and all at once.

Nestbox

See what I've made here and hung overhead

out of reach. Something of the dead
of these surrounding presences, these red cedars,
something of their grain and spread and loftiness
sawn and squared, of their fragrance. It is ingenious

protection against weather with a whole side that opens
to sky if you wish. A small nail in a slot holds it

shut. I have followed instructions and made adjustments for the years
of visitation, the favoured locations, that seem now merely

favoured minutes of the long year, those in any scant April
when the violet-green iridescence slips in

and out through the perfect oval
and the raucous chirping emerges. It's nothing new. It's everything

measured and sturdy I've handled, and emptiness
cornered, fastened upon as invitation.

The Height Of Folly

To have worked so hard at something
wisteria comes effortlessly into

and sets adrift in an off-hand fragrant gesture
of silvery mauve. To have clambered house-high
in soft air *against* disappearance. Holding to it. Knowingly.

Notes On The One Note Of The Unknown Bird

Not strange. Familiar in dawn waking, early
spring. A ring like the ring of a halyard ring
on aluminum mast at a distance, moored

in wave-rock

but lighter, hollower—and with longer pause. Almost whistle.
Each instance the same and new to itself, singular

as the smallest increment
of thought or query. Plea? Not answering.
A sort of regularity. No rhythm. (And then not missing

a beat the dilemma of attention—the trees

that leaves out, the mossed rock-faces. It *leafs* out, all ears. The whole
wending way . . .) *Hear?* Steadfast
in those vast in-betweens

what's realized, recognized, edged
up to in one's little cot, one's bit of horizontal

Dickinsonian dash into white space, white noise—almost

to the next phrase? It is of many springs, airless, airborne.
Better nameless. Having asked around, slept around
the clock, across the years within hearing without
listening, at home with it, arguably happy,
better not to know

what the one thing and nothing is asking of one
stretched out not so far as word even—

a flagging, flag-waving, occasional grace note paced over
abyss, into absurdity (possibly

not bird). That flawless something. This unfaltering
falling for it. This calling.

To The Branch From Which The Robin Flew

that bore the weight of pulse and trill and is shaking it off

that inhabits its allotted space fully in diminishing doodles

that knew from before the beginning it wouldn't be harking far
after flight and song

that in its tangential rooted inherent stillness uninterruptedly
senses elementals, and is therein expressive
but immune to lamentation

that is the lateral receptiveness of a vertical patient persistence tipped
in nonchalant fall-back from furthest untextured blue

undipped brush
of a painterly attention

at ease in the forest's grey-green foreground
at rest in the tensile essential mist of itself

A Question Of Aesthetics

Confronted by beauty, confronting beauty, what
has beauty confronted? Abstract transparent affinity

consciousness. Dream portal. Memory whiff orgasmer
polymer. Joy pulsar. Pang archive. Sad sack

of culturally programmed sensory apparatus.
Complexity symmetry capacitator in mind-wide

harmony/proportion/hue mode. Huge need
combing the data. Knotty frontal lobe of Theseus

Thesaurus Access Device (THREAD). Ingenuous
humility, the aw shucks of awe. Creator defaulting

to beholder in terror of responsibility. Open
shutter. In-breath of singer about to bite

note one. Celebrant potential
as statue, beatified. Gulf addict.

Browse

I had not meant to talk myself into silence.
I had in mind an irony honoured

that would take heart too from innocence out-
of-the-blue, as when stepping

into summer rain to cover the boat
there seems a sudden freshness in the smell of dry grass flattened
to earth. A serious wet newness. As what the young buck in the garden squandered

wasn't raspberries, but the newest leaf of next years' canes and nothing
to stretch or kneel for, only those easiest. Only the torso of the verdure, haunches

to shoulder. Body of the world. I would walk around out of my head with choosing.
Not choosing. Nibbling in a crooked light whatever caught it. I would not talk

myself into corners and conclusions. I would be whetted appetite. This would be
banquet, each piquancy mouthed leisurely, articulate, ever-furthering, fruitful only

incidentally. But see

how he wheels within enclosure at the dog's bark, outflanked
and vulnerable. Routed. Who thought himself dreaming to be the thing.

Who dreams himself speaking to be the thing.

Underberries

Until your peripheral work is exhausted, your standing work
in the easy light, and you've mastered the slight

shifts of perspective from above or aside that reveal
the fruit behind the leaves you won't even imagine

you could lie on your back in the loam and musky shade
beneath the lush foliage reaching up, feeling for them, feeling

them (plucked

just so) let go between your fingers with a subtle
resistance into your palms, settling with discrete aplomb and a sigh

of summer heat and sweetness past
their skirmish with lips and tongue

into the messy juice and stain and unshouldered weight
of satisfaction, into the shoulderless dark

of you there.

Wind Chime

Let the wind speak
        that is paradise.
                —Ezra Pound

Come sway in its ear-level lilt and lapses, fond instrument
day-long of come what may. It lolls, an insatiate

tongue for the random, whim's trinket, net
of the invisible, middle-sister to leaf

and sail, shimmering
suspension in silver wire, knotted

to waft and to the copper lizard, to the warm belly
of sleep, to the cusp and tasty metallic slither

of consciousness. Here
in the slip-stream off
a five tone scale, in

infinite range of interval, swinging from sunny
jingle to anguished cacophony, shimmies all the jazz

and dirge of weather—limitless possibility, excruciating
limitation. Here is the puffed world expansive

as the air come sidling, glancing
home to itself at a porch corner

thinly, briefly, just under the eaves. It might be
our biggest brain tinkling, immersed

in a further exquisite brilliance, that ultimately appropriate distance:
background. *Lead, accompaniment!* Lest we blunder

against you forever ducking inside for the phone . . . Let's slip/
slide sun-stunned and song-prone astray

into bodiless voice.

Cosmos

On my list so long this biggest word
it won't wait longer, insistent

(it must be) upon diminishment, dispersal
but who'd have guessed

into syllables of hue, spectra? Petals! Descending
from all manner of things, un-numbering, counting
back in mind's eye, in memory
to the single essential . . .

to fall upon this real flower indivisible, starburst

penumbra, five-petalled, an ur-rose
of bloom that occurs to me, that I recognize

oddly, portentously, as if it is the quintet
of my family, my earthly kin, my fateful
true world beyond thinking, knowing . . .

while nothing (that fine orb
in hot pursuit of an ultimate horizon)
adds up to quite true sum, won't easily
round off, O still unravish'd

bride of quietness, bride of the one god, mind zest, you
pure zero of the possible, invisible bud . . .
Infinitely, recklessly

superfluous, late in the year, past high summer and its turn
and twists of numinous colour chasing
itself in the molecules, cosmos
self-seeded throughout the east border sang
my banns to these shorter, fewer days, to this resolute anemone, wind-

flower, pinkish grey of sunset-cloud over
the strait, aspect of your cheek at twilight, your thigh
in the haze of my touch. That's the moody poise

I'm given, wanting. Essence and bedrock. Skin-cool, smoke-soft
bloom in the void, immaculate in solar wind, in south-easterlies (even seething

in my brine, in my sea of misnomers, miscalculations) still
to appear and remain with me, here: open hand at the foot

of the stairs on its stalk of chance from the whisky-barrel planter, plausible fleck
and flourish of the whole. Here I might not, headlong, heedless, fall

but lose my footing, my timing, nearly unnoticed
and recover on the granite where the lawn ends. And laugh

at this tangle of unspooled presumption, elaborate
meander. Say clumsiness. Say

only human. And my last word and weathered
opportunity a viable absolute after all.
Almost absolution.

Notes & Acknowledgements

Many of these poems, some in earlier versions, have appeared or will appear in the following periodicals and anthologies: *BC Studies; Canadian Literature; Capilano Review; drunkenboat (US); Event; Grain; Last Repository; Moving Worlds (UK); Prism International; Saving Trees, Saving Wildwood; Wascana Review.*

Thanks to Carmen Elliot for permission to use her photo, Bumblebee on St John's Wort, as cover image.

Across the lawn of Marvell's high-summer invocation, I'm grateful for the contemplative shade cast by the opening lines of John Ashbery's poem, "Late Echo" (*As We Know*, Penguin, 1979).

The inscription to "nowrite.doc" is from Jorie Graham's poem "Spelled From The Shadows Aubade" (*The Errancy*, Ecco Press, 1997).

Ezra Pound's heavenly city, Dioce, appears in *The Pisan Cantos*, and Hart Crane's "visionary company" in his poem "The Broken Tower".

"Airing The Bed" is after (if not in the midst of, an interruption of) Jack Gilbert's poem "Breakfast" (*Monolithos*, Graywolf, 1984).

"Owl Clover" and "Hallowell" are for Solveigh and Joe Harrison, respectively.

"Notes On The One Note Of The Unknown Bird" is for Don McKay.

The numbers in "Cosmos" belong to Blake, the echoes to Keats.

Special thanks to Ursula Vaira at Leaf Press for the chapbook, *nowrite.doc*, to Anik See at Fox Run Press for the forthcoming chapbook *Twinned Towers*, and to Nancy McLean at Pooka Press for broadsheets of "A Kiss Beneath Wisteria", "Insignificance" and "Inheritance".

"Trumpet Vine" and "Stationery Almond" first appeared as broadsheets printed by the poet at High Ground Press, the former in celebration of his 50th birthday, and the latter as a housewarming gift for Barbara and Douglas Lambert.

Thanks to the Canada Council for assistance to the poet in the writing of this book.

About The Poet

John Pass was born in 1947 in Sheffield, England and has lived in Canada since 1953. He has a BA in English from the University of British Columbia (1969) and teaches at Capilano College in Sechelt and North Vancouver. He is the author of fifteen books and chapbooks and his poems have appeared in numerous magazines and anthologies in Canada, and abroad. In 1988 he won the Canada Poetry Prize. He has won awards from The League of Canadian Poets, The BC Federation of Writers and The BC Arts Council, and has been nominated for a National Magazine Award. Pass was the recipient in 2001 of the Gillian Lowndes Award. Two previous books, *The Hour's Acropolis* and *Water Stair,* were short listed for The Dorothy Livesay Poetry Prize. *Water Stair* was also short listed for the Governor General's Award. John Pass lives near Sakinaw Lake on BC's Sunshine Coast with his wife, writer Theresa Kishkan.